POL

the most poetic person

22

ORCHARD BOOKS
96 Leonard Street, London EC2A 4RH
Orchard Books Australia
14 Mars Road, Lane Cove, NSW 2066
Text © Laurence Anholt 1997
Illustrations © Tony Ross 1997
First published in Great Britain in 1997
First paperback publication 1998
A CIP catalogue record for this book is available from the
British Library.
1 86039 554 6 (hardback)
1 86039 626 7 (paperback)
Printed in Great Britain

POLLY
the most poetic person

Laurence Anholt
Illustrated by Tony Ross

 ORCHARD BOOKS

We are going to meet Polly.
We are going to meet Polly, the
most poetic person on the whole
planet. No matter how she tries,
Polly can't stop making poems.
"*Any time*
Is rhyme time," says Polly.

As soon as Polly wakes up in the morning, she starts to rhyme...
"*Poems in the bedroom, poems in the shower,*
Poems in the kitchen, hour after hour.

When I have my breakfast or
when I flush the loo,
I like poems all the time with
everything I do."

Polly loved her poems. But her
friends began to get cross. "Please,
Polly, no more poems!" they said.

Polly tried to get a job, but no one
wanted a poet in a supermarket...
"Mustard, custard, carrots, peas,
Thank you, Madam,
Five pounds please."

Polly tried to get a job in a school.
But no one wanted a rhyming
Lollipop Lady...
"*Hurry children, don't delay,
A great big lorry is coming this
way.*"

Polly tried to get a job in the police force. But no one wanted a poetic police woman...
"Stop! Stop! You naughty pest, Drop that loot. You're under arrest."

So Polly sat at home all alone…
"*No one wants me,*
It makes me sad,
People think my poems are bad."

Polly was a lonely poet. But she couldn't stop rhyming. At last, Polly went to see a clever doctor.

The doctor's name was
Doctor Bill.
*"Doctor Bill, will you give
me a pill?
I can't stop rhyming.
It's making me ill."*

Doctor Bill looked inside Polly's
mouth. "Open wide," he said.
"Say, 'Aah'!"
"Aah. Bah. Far. Star.
Seven monkeys in a car."

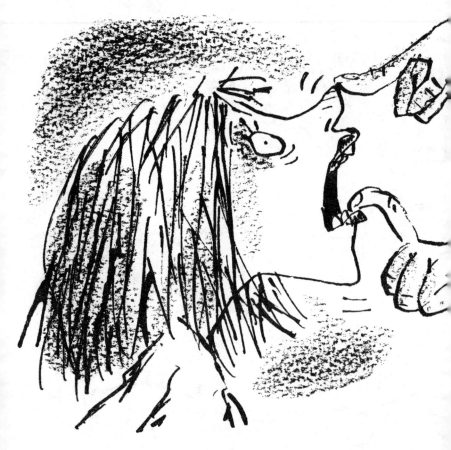

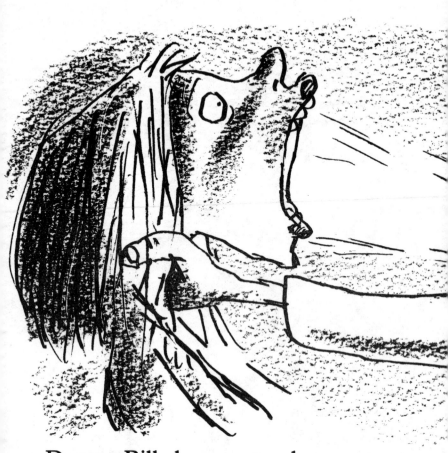

Doctor Bill shone a torch
inside Polly's mouth.
"Say, 'Ooh'!" he said.
"*Ooh, too. To-wit to-woo.
Nine owls in a stew.*"

"Yes," said Doctor Bill. "A bad case of rhyming. I'm afraid there is no cure. I hope no one else will catch it. Next patient please."

BEWARE
OF
SPOTS

So Polly started to walk slowly
home. She felt sadder than ever.

"It's a lonely life,
When you're a poet.
I've always guessed it,
Now I know it."

Polly walked past a big factory. A
sign said:
'THE HAPPY BIRTHDAY
CARD FACTORY'.

But the people inside the factory were not happy at all. They could make nice birthday cards but they

could not write poems to go inside
them...

'*I hope your birthday is full of fun,*
Bright and warm just like
the...er...um...'

The people in the factory
couldn't rhyme at all. Polly
knocked at the door...

*"Knock, knock, excuse me please,
I could write your poems with
ease."*

Polly had lots of ideas for
birthday poems…

Your birthday comes just
once a year
be sure to smile
from ear to ear.

'Happy birthday, darling sister,
I like you more than a nasty
blister.'

'Granny, your eyes are bright and twinkly,
With every year you get more wrinkly.'

'Tomatoes are red and
Violets are blue,
From Polly the Poet –
Happy Birthday to you!'

Everyone at the Happy Birthday Card Factory began to clap.

They thought Polly was the best poet in the world.

They asked if she would like a job
at the Happy Birthday Card
Factory.

"*Thank you, thank you,*
I'd love to stay,

And write my poems every day."
So Polly the Poet stayed for ever
at the Happy Birthday Card
Factory. And everyone loved her.

Each year Polly sent a special birthday poem to Doctor Bill. She was glad he hadn't made her better.

Doctor Bill liked the card but he didn't really need the poem. He had too many poems already.

Because Doctor Bill had caught
Polly's rhyming...
*"Take one of these,
if you cough or sneeze,*

*You'll soon feel better,
Next patient please!"*